10116

ELVES

JOEL NEWSOME

Cavendish
Square

New York

CREATURES OF FANTASY

ELVES

BY

JOEL NEWSOME

CAVENDISH SQUARE PUBLISHING · NEW YORK

Published in 2017 by Cavendish Square Publishing, LLC
243 5th Avenue, Suite 136, New York, NY 10016

Website: cavendishsq.com

This publication represents the opinions and views of the author based on his or her personal experience, knowledge, and
research. The information in this book serves as a general guide only. The author and publisher have used their best efforts in
preparing this book and disclaim liability rising directly or indirectly from the use and application of this book.

CPSIA Compliance Information: Batch #CS16CSQ

All websites were available and accurate when this book was sent to press.

Library of Congress Cataloging-in-Publication Data

Names: Newsome, Joel, 1984- author.
Title: Elves / Joel Newsome.
Description: New York : Cavendish Square Publishing, [2017] |
Series: Creatures of fantasy | Includes bibliographical references and index.
Identifiers: LCCN 2016000268 (print) | LCCN 2016006081 (ebook) |
ISBN 9781502618528 (library bound) | ISBN 9781502618535 (ebook)
Subjects: LCSH: Elves--Juvenile literature.
Classification: LCC GR549 .N49 2017 (print) | LCC GR549 (ebook) |
DDC 398.21--dc23
LC record available at http://lccn.loc.gov/2016000268

Editorial Director: David McNamara
Editor: Kristen Susienka
Copy Editor: Rebecca Rohan
Art Director: Jeffrey Talbot
Designer: Amy Greenan
Production Assistant: Karol Szymczuk
Photo Research: J8 Media

The photographs in this book are used by permission and through the courtesy of:
Sir Joseph Noel Paton(1821-1901)/Art Gallery and Museum, Kelvingrove, Glasgow, Scotland/© Culture and Sport Glasgow (Museums)/
Bridgeman Images, 2-3; Mary Evans Picture Library, 6, 11, 26; British Library, London, UK/© British Library Board. All Rights Reserved/
Bridgeman Images, 8; balenabianca/iStock/Thinkstock.com, 13; Warner Brother/JK Rowling/Ronald Grant Archive/Mary Evans Picture
Library, 14; Ullstein bild/ullstein bild via Getty Images, 16; Author Unknown/Septentrionalen Regionum Descript. Abraham Ortelius.
Antwerpen, late 16th century/File: 16th century map of Scandinavia.jpg/Wikimedia Commons, 18; Richard of Haldingham (Richard de Bello)
(fl.c.1260-1305)/Hereford Cathedral, Herefordshire, UK/Bridgeman Images, 20; English School, (19th century)/Private Collection/© Look
and Learn/Valerie Jackson Harris Collection/ Bridgeman Images, 21; 7831/Gamma-Rapho via Getty Images, 30; British Library, London,
UK/© British Library Board. All Rights Reserved/Bridgeman Images, 31; Smart and tidy boys are we, illustration from 'The Poor Cobbler' in
'Reading Aright' Book I, by James H. Steel (colour litho), Jacobs, Helen (1888-1970)/Private Collection/Bridgeman Images, 32; ZU_09/E+/
Getty Images, 35; Culture Club/Hulton Archive/Getty Images, 36; Ivy Close Images/Alamy Stock Photo, 37; Everett Collection/Alamy Stock
Photo, 40; Sullivan, William Holmes (1836-1908)/Private Collection/Photo © Christie's Images/Bridgeman Images, 42; andere andrea petrlik/
Shutterstock.com, 45; Celiafoto/Shutterstock.com, 46; Greg Benz/Moment/Getty Images, 47; Brewtnall, Edward Frederick (1846-1902)/©
Trustees of the Royal Watercolour Society, London, UK/Bridgeman Images, 48; AF archive/Alamy Stock Photo, 54; Rankin Bass/Screenshot
from from Rudolph the Red-Nosed Reindeer/File: Hermey the elf and Rudolph.jpg/Wikimedia Commons, 57.

Printed in the United States of America

CONTENTS

INTRODUCTION

Elves, such as Denmark's Nisse, love dancing and music.

Since the first humans walked Earth, myths and legends have engaged minds and inspired imaginations. Ancient civilizations used stories to explain phenomena in the world around them, such as the weather, the tides, and natural disasters. As different cultures evolved, so too did their stories. From their traditions and observations emerged creatures with powerful abilities, mythical intrigue, and their own origins. Sometimes, different cultures encouraged various manifestations of the same creature. At other times, these creatures morphed into entirely new beings with greater powers than their predecessors.

Today, societies still celebrate the folklore of their ancestors—on-screen in TV shows and movies such as *Doctor Who, Once Upon a Time,* and *Star Wars,* and in books such as the *Harry Potter* and *Twilight* series. Some of these creatures existed, while others are merely myth.

In the Creatures of Fantasy series, we celebrate captivating stories of the past from all around the world. Each book focuses on creatures both familiar and unknown: the elusive alien, the grumpy troll, the devious demon, the graceful elf, the spellbinding wizard, and the harrowing mummy. Their various incarnations throughout history are brought to life. All have their own origins, their own legends, and their own influences on the imagination today. Each story adds a new perspective to the human experience and encourages people to revisit tales of the past in order to understand their presence in the modern age.

The Elf-King asleep.

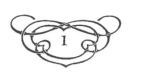

TINY PEOPLE, HIDDEN HOUSES

"Every elf and fairy sprite
Hop as light as bird from brier;
And this ditty after me
Sing, and dance it trippingly."
WILLIAM SHAKESPEARE, *A MIDSUMMER NIGHT'S DREAM*

NE OF THE MOST CURIOUS AND conflated creatures in human mythology is the elf. When you think of elves, you might think of Santa Claus's helpers at the North Pole or J. R. R. Tolkien's creatures in the Lord of the Rings series. However, elven creatures have been illustrated through fairy tales and myths for centuries, long before the creation of Middle Earth or the modern celebration of Christmas. A variety of cultures tell tales regarding elves. They come in a variety of shapes and sizes. As a result, their likeness and attributes bear similarities to fairies, gnomes, dwarves, and trolls. In some instances, these related creatures are also called "elves."

Opposite: Some elves are said to be as tiny as insects.

However, over the centuries, a modern idea of the elf has evolved and given the creature its own personality and appearance.

The most popular image of the elf is a small, pale-skinned, pointy-eared being that looks much like a tiny human. While most myths describe elves as being small, their actual size varies from being slightly smaller than human beings to being small enough to live within the folds of a rose petal, as in Hans Christian Andersen's tale, "The Elf of the Rose." Clothing worn by these creatures ranges from **homely** rags to beautiful garments, depending on where the story originates.

Scandinavian folklore draws several considerable distinctions between male and female elves with regard to appearance and personality. In *The World Guide to Gnomes, Fairies, Elves, and Other Little People*, author Thomas Keightley details Danish *Elle*-people:

> The appearance of the man is that of an old man with a low-crowned hat on his head; the Elle-woman is young and of a fair and attractive countenance, but behind she is hollow … Young men should be especially on their guard against her, for it is very difficult to resist her; and she has, moreover, a stringed instrument, which, when she plays on it, quite ravishes their hearts. The man may be often seen near the Elle-moors, bathing himself in the sunbeams, but if anyone comes too near him, he opens his mouth wide and breathes upon them, and his breath produces sickness and pestilence. But the women are frequently to be seen by moonshine; then they dance their rounds in the high grass so lightly and so gracefully, that they seldom meet a denial when they offer their hand to a rash young man.

A Christmas Tradition

In the Western world, we often associate elves with the Christmas holiday. Widespread belief holds that elves live at the North Pole and work in Santa's workshop. There, they make toys for all the world's children to receive on Christmas morning. While European tales of elves assisting Father Christmas (Santa) have been told for centuries, the modern American idea of the elf as Santa's worker is fairly new. This version of elves was first popularized by an anonymous poem published in *Harper's Weekly* in 1857:

Elves help Santa Claus bring Christmas joy to children all over the world.

In his house upon the top of a hill / And almost out of sight / He keeps a great many elves at work / All working with all their might / To make a million of pretty things / Cakes, sugar-plums, and toys, / To fill the stockings, hung up you know / By the little girls and boys.

This poem gave Americans the **basis** of the Christmas elf image. It has been added to by a variety of movies, toys, and games since.

The poem also lends another idea that has continued with the modern perception of elves: secrecy and staying out of sight of humans:

But the queer old man when a stranger comes, / Orders every elf to stop; / And the house, and work, and workmen all / Instantly take a twist, / And just you may think you are there, / They are off in a frosty mist.

The quality of being hidden and secretive was not specific to Christmas elves. **Obscurity**, mystery, and sometimes even invisibility are common aspects of all elf myths. This is especially true when it comes to elven homes.

HIDDEN DWELLINGS

Often elves are described as living in hidden, protected places. Some reside underground or in tiny caves carved into cliffsides. Others live among humans or inside plants. Some stories even discuss a fairy realm, beyond the human world, where many elves live. Very few humans get to enter the fairy world, but those who do are often rewarded with great riches and sights of great wealth and celebration.

When a human gains entry to an elf dwelling, it is usually because they are being rewarded for some good deed. Sometimes, this reward comes as a complete surprise. For instance, in one ancient tale from Iceland, a man is walking at night, lost in a snowstorm, and happens upon a row of lit, beautiful houses. He knocks on one of the doors, and its inhabitants welcome him inside. They make him a guest of honor, offering him delicious food and wine. The next morning the man eats an even more delicious breakfast and the head of the house gives him many gifts, including cakes for his children and a cloak for his wife. The man is astonished at his host's generosity, but the host insists that the gifts are tokens of gratitude. He then tells the man

This ordinary-looking stump could house a whole kingdom of elves!

of how he had **inadvertently** saved his son's life. He explains that one day the man had been standing with a group of other men who were throwing stones against a large rock. The man had told them to stop throwing stones, and though they chided him, they eventually relented. The elf's son had been up all night and was sleeping beneath the rock that was being pelted by stones. If the man had not prevented the stone throwers, his son surely would have been killed.

Household Duties

While elves generally live in hidden places, there are many stories of elves being employed by humans. Mostly, elves serve as farmhands or household servants. These workers are usually female. They are particular about keeping things tidy and can complete seemingly impossible chores at an extraordinary pace, without help. They sometimes live with the humans they work for but are often very secretive about their comings and goings. They also do not let on that they are, in fact, elves. If an elf's identity is ever discovered, they are likely to vanish, never to be seen again by their human employer.

House elves like Dobby from the Harry Potter books and movies are tasked with cleaning up after humans.

Changing Association with Christmas

Today, elves are associated with helping Santa Claus prepare for Christmas, but in ancient tales, elves often did not participate in human Christmas traditions. In many stories, house servant elves refuse to go to church on Christmas Eve with the rest of the servants and instead go back to their dwellings for a large feast with other elves.

In some stories, elves play mischievous tricks on humans during the holidays. There is a Scandinavian tale that tells of a crossroads where four different churches can be seen at the end of each road. It is said that if you sit in the middle of the intersection on Christmas Eve, elves will surround you from every direction and tempt you with gold, treasures, and delicious foods, but you must not speak or accept the gifts. If you pass that test, elf women will surround you and take the form of your mother, sisters, and other relatives begging you to follow them. If you are still able to resist, and you make it to the first light of dawn without speaking, you must then yell, "Praise be to God! His daylight fills the heavens!" As soon as the elves hear this they will vanish and leave all the goods they have tried to tempt you with, which you will then be free to take. If you fail to resist the elves and speak or accept their gifts, legend has it that you will go mad.

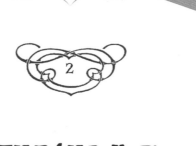

VIKING ROOTS

"Say knowest thou the Elves' gay and joyous race?
The banks of streams are their home;
They spin of the moonshine their holiday-dress,
With their lily-white hands frolicsome."
ERIK JOHAN STAGNELIUS

A S WITH MANY CREATURES THAT
originally appear in ancient lore, the earliest representation
of elves is impossible to pinpoint exactly, but the majority
of ancient elf stories come from Norse mythology. The **Norsemen**
were people who lived between the ninth and eleventh centuries CE
and spoke Old Norse, an ancient language. Norsemen originated
in what is now Sweden, Norway, Denmark, Finland, Iceland, and
Greenland. Many Norsemen were farmers and fishermen, but
their landscapes were often harsh and infertile. As a result, many
Norsemen adopted the Viking way of life and became expert
sailors and traders. Some became bodyguards employed by foreign
kings, while others were ruthless pirates. Vikings traveled to many

Opposite:
Vikings were hardy,
seafaring people.

A sixteenth-century map of ancient Scandinavia.

different countries and thus their mythology spread throughout the world. Some places that were rich with Norse myth are present-day Sweden, Denmark, Norway, Iceland, Northern Germany, Scotland, and England.

Norse Mythology Begins

The Norsemen often lived in **inhospitable** lands filled with ice and snow. This treacherous terrain heavily influenced their folklore. Many of their stories take place in desolate areas and involve gods or goddesses that use the elements as ways to weaken their enemies or gain an advantage in conflict.

The Norsemen believed that before the world existed there were only two places: the North and the South. The North was filled with ice and snow and was called Niflheim. It was the world of the dead. The South was full of flames and was called Muspelheim. The space between Niflheim and Muspelheim was an emptiness known as Ginnungagap. Eventually, it was here that the human world would be created. Icy rivers flowed from Niflheim through Ginnungagap. As these frozen rivers crept closer to Muspelheim, they began to melt. The melting rivers eventually formed a giant. From this creature came the creation of elves.

Ymir and Audumla

To understand the origins of elves, one must first look to the Norse myth of the world's first creatures. Formed from the melting drops of ice, they were known as Frost Giants. The first Frost Giant, Ymir, was formed along with a giant cow, Audumla. To survive, Ymir drank the milk of Audumla. The cow, meanwhile, was sustained by licking the salty ice. As Ymir slept, his perspiration created more Frost Giants. One day, when Audumla was licking the ice, a large manlike form began to surface. Over the next three days Audumla licked the shape free from the ice. This figure was Buri, who eventually had a son, Bor, who married a Frost Giantess called Bestla. Bestla gave birth to three sons who became the first gods, Odin, Vili, and Ve.

Ymir was furious about the existence of Buri and his descendants, and he, along with his fellow giants, waged war on them. The war dragged on with neither side gaining much advantage until Bor, Odin, Vili, and Ve killed Ymir. Ymir's blood was said to pour out of him with such force that it drowned all the other giants except one, who escaped and lived to create more like himself.

After slaying Ymir, Odin, Vili, and Ve dragged his body into Ginnungagap and used Ymir's corpse to create the world. His flesh became the earth while his blood and sweat formed the rivers and oceans. Ymir's bones and teeth were made into hills and cliffs. His hair became the plants and trees. The gods used his skull as the dome of the sky and his brains were thrown into the air to serve as

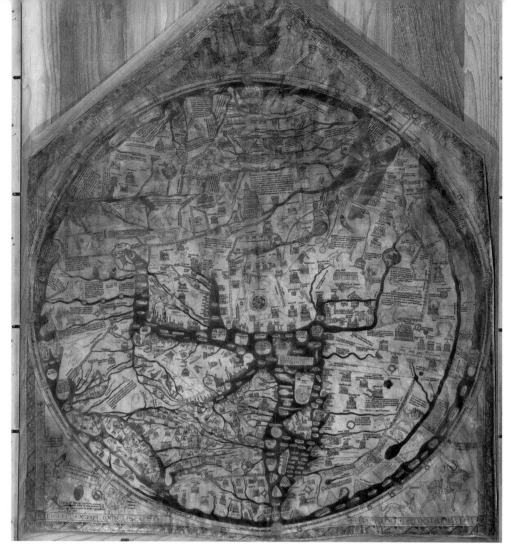

A thirteenth-century map of the world.

clouds. They then took flames from Muspelheim and threw them into the sky to create the stars, sun, and moon.

The Creation of Elves

While the gods were creating the world, many maggot-like creatures had been growing in the flesh of Ymir. Seeing these vulgar creatures, the Norse gods decided to bestow superhuman intelligence on them and divided them into two groups—those that were devious and cunning and those that were benevolent and good. Dark elves comprised the first group, while light elves made up the latter.

Dark Elves

Dark elves, also referred to in many tales as dwarves, came to live underground in a place called Svartalfheim. They were excellent craftsmen, and many Norse myths detail dwarves making weapons and jewelry for various gods. One such tale tells the story of the creation of Sif's golden hair. Sif, the wife of the god Thor, had a magnificent head of hair. It reached from the top of her head to her feet and was the color of golden grain. Thor was very proud of his wife's hair. One morning, he awoke to find

Elves are sometimes mischievous!

that someone had shaved Sif's head bald in the night! Thor knew the perpetrator to be Loki, a trickster and the embodiment of evil in Norse mythology. He went in search of him and once found, Loki begged forgiveness as Thor choked the life from him. Thor only relented when Loki promised to get Sif a new head of hair as fine and abundant as her own hair had been.

Desperate, Loki fled to Svartalfheim. He begged a dwarf named Dvalin to make both the luxurious hair for Sif and an offering for Odin, the supreme god, and Frey, the god of sunshine. Dvalin granted Loki's request. He made the spear, Gungnir, which never missed its target, and a ship called *Skidbladnir*. The ship could sail through the air as well as on water, and while it could hold the gods and all their horses, it could be folded small enough to fit inside a pocket. He likewise spun a new head of hair for Sif. The hair was made from the finest golden thread and would grow naturally as soon as it touched her head.

Loki, overjoyed by these offerings, declared Dvalin the cleverest of craftsmen. Brock, another dwarf, overheard Loki's exclamation and wagered that his brother Sindri could make three gifts that would surpass Dvalin's. Loki accepted the challenge and bet his life against Brock's that Sindri would not be able to produce finer gifts than Dvalin had. It was agreed that whoever lost the bet would have to lose his head.

The brothers worked together to accomplish the task, Brock crafting the golden objects while Sindri went out to gather magical powers. Brock worked diligently, while Loki, hoping to slow Brock's pace, turned himself into a gadfly and stung Brock's hand. The dwarf continued despite the pain. When Sindri returned, he unveiled a large boar called Gullinbursti, which had golden bristles that radiated light and could fly great distances in an instant.

Next, Brock threw some gold into a flame, while Sindri gathered powers for the object. Loki stung Brock again, this time on the cheek. Brock worked on and removed the magic ring called Draupnir from the fire when Sindri returned. Exhausted, Sindri collapsed into a deep sleep as Brock crafted the final gift.

Loki again attacked, stinging Brock on his brow with such force that blood gushed from the wound. The blood obscured Brock's vision momentarily. It took only an instant, but he was distracted long enough for the final object, a hammer, to be malformed. Nonetheless, Brock was confident in the gifts he and his brother had created and did not hesitate to deliver them

to the gods. He gave Odin the ring Draupnir, Frey the boar Gullinbursti, and Thor the hammer with the shortened handle called Miölnir.

Shortly after, Loki delivered the spear Gungnir to Odin, the ship *Skidbladnir* to Frey, and the golden hair to Thor. Although the gods agreed Sif's new hair was just as luminous as her own hair had been, they announced that Brock had won the wager. Seeing that he had lost the gamble, Loki immediately fled but was recaptured by Thor. Thor delivered Loki to the dwarves so they could take their revenge but stipulated that they could not harm his neck. Unable to decapitate Loki, the dwarves settled on sewing Loki's lips shut.

Agents of Love and Light

While the dark elves were principally craftsmen who dwelled underground, the light elves were **charitable** spirits that obeyed Frey's every command. Frey ruled their kingdom, Alfheim, and for that the light elves dedicated their lives. Light elves did good deeds and served in the interests of love and laughter. One example of the light elf commitment to **benevolence** in the service of love is the tale of the wooing of a woman named Gerda.

One day, Frey ventured to Odin's throne and looked out over all creation. Gazing toward the North, Frey saw a beautiful young woman, Gerda, entering the house of a frost giant. Frey fell instantly in love and wandered back to Alfheim in a fog. His father, Niord, noticed Frey's melancholy and asked Skirnir, a servant of Frey, to find out what plagued his son. After much convincing, Frey finally related his love for Gerda and his despair that she was a relative of the frost giants. Skirnir offered to woo Gerda in Frey's name, as

long as he could use Frey's horse and receive Frey's magical sword, which fought of its own accord once it was drawn from its sheath. Frey agreed.

Before departing, Skirnir stole an image of Frey's face from a reflection in a nearby brook. Armed with the portrait, the magical ring Draupnir, and eleven golden apples, Skirnir rode off to the dwelling of the frost giant in order to woo Gerda. A fire burned around the house, protecting it from intruders, but Skirnir simply set his spurs into Frey's horse and rode through the flames. In the presence of Gerda, he explained his reasons for visiting, showed her the stolen reflection of Frey's likeness, and offered her the golden apples as well as the magic ring. Gerda, however, refused the offerings. Angered at her refusal, Skirnir then threatened to cut off her head with his magic sword. Gerda again rebuffed his advances made in Frey's name. Finally, Skirnir resorted to magic. He conjured a spell and told her that unless she yielded to Frey's wishes and married him, she would endure eternal celibacy or marry an old frost giant, whom she would never truly love. Finally, Gerda relented and agreed to marry Frey in nine nights. Despite Gerda's initial hesitance, she and Frey lived happily together as a result of Skirnir's persistence.

The Origin of Echoes

Dark elves were not just incredible craftsmen; they were also playful and discreet. While they are said to have supplied the Norse gods with a variety of weapons and treasures, they are also said to be the reason one hears an echo while in an underground cave.

According to legend, these beings can transport themselves with astonishing speed and often hide behind rocks, where they playfully repeat the last words of a conversation that they overhear. As a result, in some areas, echoes have become known as "dwarf talk."

It is reasoned that people never see where the sound comes from because each dwarf has a small red hat called a **Tarnkappe**, which makes the wearer invisible. It is said that the dark elves do not dare appear above the surface of the earth without their Tarnkappe, otherwise they will be turned to stone. As long as the dark elves wear their Tarnkappes, they remain unseen and safe from this terrible fate.

MAGICAL LITTLE PEOPLE

"I met a little Elfman once,
Down where the lilies blow.
I asked him why he was so small,
And why he didn't grow."

JOHN KENDRICK BANGS, "THE LITTLE ELF"

THROUGHOUT MANY DIFFERENT CULTURES, elves have a variety of magical abilities. These abilities range from dream travel to incredible speed to the ability to affect the dreams of humans. Much like their appearances, their powers vary from myth to myth and from culture to culture.

DREAM PLAY

One common trait elves supposedly possess is the ability to affect humans' dreams. In some myths, elves can narrate dreams by whispering in the ear of a sleeping person. An example of this appears in Hans Christian Andersen's "The Elf of the Rose." This tale tells the story of a tiny elf who lives in the petals of a rose.

Opposite: Dreams allow elves to communicate with sleeping humans.

One day, he is suddenly transported from his home when a young maiden plucks his rose and gives it to her suitor as a gift. It is her way of asking him to remember her on a long voyage he is about to take. The maiden places the rose in her suitor's shirt pocket. With nowhere else to go, the elf tries to sleep. However, the noise of the suitor's beating heart is too loud and prevents him from doing so.

Meanwhile, the suitor is on his way home. While walking, he encounters the maiden's villainous brother, who despises the suitor. Her brother kills the suitor and beheads him, burying the body and head in a clearing. During the killing, the elf is able to hide in a furled leaf that has fallen upon the killer's head. He is carried back to the home that the maiden and her brother share. As the brother looks in on his sister, the leaf falls onto her bed.

The elf whispers the details of the crime and directions to her lover's grave into her ear, and adds that she will find a withered leaf on her bed when she awakens, so she will know it was not just a dream. Upon waking, the maiden finds the leaf and knows the dream was real.

That night she slips out to discover her lover's body. She digs up his grave and weeps at the sight of him. Though she longs to take his body home with her, she settles on taking his head, which she places in a pot and covers with dirt. She plants a twig of jasmine in it so that it will not look suspicious. The elf finds a nearby rose to inhabit, and every day he flies to the window of the maiden and finds her weeping by her flowerpot. Her tears fall upon the jasmine twig and each day as she grows paler and weaker, the plant grows greener and stronger. One day the elf visits and finds her sleeping by her flowerpot. He sits by her ear and talks of her suitor's beating heart on the night of his death, the sweet smell of

the rose, and other elven delights. The maiden dreams sweetly and gently drifts off to death to be with her love. At that moment, the jasmine blooms.

Traveling Elves

Other myths detail humans traveling with elves to their kingdoms while they are dreaming. One such fairy tale comes from Iceland and tells of a young noblewoman named Katla. She falls asleep while her husband is away and sleeps for four days and four nights. On the fifth day, she awakens in a state of deep sadness. Her husband returns and notices the change in her behavior. He asks her servants about it, and they tell him only that she has slept for four days. He then asks Katla, when they are alone, what the reason is for her demeanor. Katla explains that a beautiful woman in expensive clothes came to her bedside and asked her to travel back with the woman to the farm where Katla once lived. As Katla complied, the woman placed a pair of gloves in Katla's bed, saying that they would take her place while she was away. The woman kidnapped Katla and took her to an island with a magnificent castle on it. She tried to persuade Katla to become the queen of this beautiful kingdom by marrying the king. Katla refused and was only released when she agreed to name her firstborn son after the elven king. All of this comes to pass while Katla is seemingly sleeping. She awakes to find the treasures the elves gave her lying in her bed.

Incredible Speed

Many stories about elves tell of how they work or travel at great speeds. In the Icelandic tale "Who Built Reynir Church," a bishop orders a farmer to build a church near his farm. However, the

farmer has great difficulty finding timber and workers. He worries he will not finish the church before winter.

One day as he is contemplating his dilemma, a strange little man approaches him and offers to build the barn himself. The farmer is overjoyed and asks his price. The man replies that he will build it for free if the farmer can figure out his name. If not, the farmer must give him his six-year-old son. The farmer eagerly agrees to the wager and is disheartened when he sees how fast the little stranger works. In spite of the man's swift work, the farmer discovers his name just before the church is finished.

Tolkien's Elves

Legolas is one of J. R. R. Tolkien's bravest elves.

You may have heard of or seen Peter Jackson's film trilogy *The Lord of the Rings*. These films are based upon books written by author J. R. R. Tolkien in 1954. Elves play a significant part in both the films and novels.

In Tolkien's books, elves are the first descendants of the Creator. Their spirits are said to be bound to the earth, and so they are meant to last as long as the earth exists. This makes elves immortal, unless they are killed by mortal means, such as in war or from deep sorrow. Tolkien's elves are specifically described as being more beautiful, graceful, skilled, and taller than humans. Their eyes are typically grey in color and able to see great distances. Elves also tend to have excellent hearing and can sometimes read minds. Some of Tolkien's elves have the gift of **clairvoyance**, or the ability to see the future. Many of the elves are skilled archers. It is perhaps Tolkien's elves that have influenced many modern perceptions of elves: fair-haired, graceful, and attractive.

Soldier Elves

Some myths characterize elves as royal soldiers. There is a legend in Denmark that elven kings keep watch over the country from cliffs that jut out over the sea. Whenever the country is threatened by war, they are said to be seen drawing up their armies near the seas and keeping watch over the waters for approaching enemies. Another tale tells of an elven king with a magnificent chariot pulled by four black horses. When he rides over the seas from one cliff to another, the waters grow black and his horses can be heard snorting and neighing. The notion of soldier elves inspired the science fiction writer Philip K. Dick to pen his short story "King of the Elves." Published in 1953, this modern fairy tale features a downtrodden elf platoon seeking refuge with their wounded king. They beg a lonely gas station owner to help them, and he is soon recruited to assist in their fight against evil forces. As the story unfolds, he realizes the extent to which their worlds overlap and that he is all too familiar with their enemy. Another popular fighting elf is Legolas of the *Lord of the Rings* trilogy. Legolas is recruited to accompany Frodo Baggins in his quest to destroy a magical ring. He is gifted with excellent eyesight and hearing and is also an expert archer who dispatches arrows with astonishing speed. It would seem that the image of the elf as a warrior would conflict with those myths that define elves as kind little cherubs. However, whenever elves appear in stories as soldiers they are portrayed as fighting a battle of good versus evil and are always on the side of nobility.

A TALE OF SECRET BENEVOLENCE AND GRATITUDE

"'What think you if we were to stay up to-night
to see who it is that lends us this helping hand?'"
THE SHOEMAKER, *THE SHOEMAKER AND THE ELVES*

MOST TALES ABOUT ELVES DESCRIBE them as secretive beings, either as a result of their size, quickness, or ability to control whether or not they are visible. These cunning creatures are often told to be helpful and resourceful with happy spirits, wanting nothing in return. A myth that bridges both ancient tales of elves and our modern-day understanding is "The Shoemaker and the Elves," told by the brothers Grimm.

The Brothers Grimm: A Firm Foundation

The brothers Grimm were two German folklorists named Jacob and Wilhelm Grimm. They collected a number of German

Opposite: The shoemaker's elves try on their new clothes.

folktales in the early 1800s. Much of our modern understanding of myths reflects the stories they published years ago. Mary Hunt translated the brothers' work into English in 1884 and included three tales of elves in a section entitled, simply, "The Elves." The other two tales in the section are short glimpses of elves interacting with humans, but "The Shoemaker and the Elves" contains a majority of the elf characteristics often conjured when one thinks of the tiny creatures.

The Shoemaker and the Elves

This tale begins with a shoemaker living in poverty. He is so poor that he cannot afford supplies to make his shoes and has only enough leather to make one more pair of shoes. In the evening, he cuts the leather in preparation for his next morning's work. He lays down in bed, says his prayers, and drifts off to sleep. The next morning he rises early and is all set to begin his work when he approaches his workbench and sees the shoes he was planning on making that day there, totally finished. He is perplexed and begins to examine the shoes.

He notices that every stitch is in the right place, and the shoes are something of a masterpiece. Not long after the shoemaker finishes his inspection, a customer walks in. The customer thinks the shoes are expertly made as well and pays more than the asking price for the shoes. The shoemaker is overjoyed; with the extra money he is able to purchase enough leather for two more pairs of shoes.

Again he cuts the leather, goes to bed, and in the morning he is excited to begin his work. Once again, the shoemaking has already been done for him. Sitting on his workbench are two more pairs of expertly made shoes. Again he inspects the shoes, and again

Wilhelm and
Jacob Grimm
popularized many
modern fairy tales.

The shoemaker and his wife discover that their helpers are elves!

he finds them remarkable. Customers are also delighted with the fine craftsmanship, and the shoemaker ends the day with enough money to buy leather for four pairs of shoes.

The pattern continues. After several weeks of this, the shoemaker becomes a wealthy man. Shortly before Christmas that same year, the man is cutting leather for shoes and has an idea. He suggests to his wife that they stay awake that night to see who their helpers are. His wife loves the idea, and they light a candle and hide behind some clothes in a corner of the room. They watch and wait.

At the stroke of midnight, two jolly, naked, little men dance over to the shoemaker's workbench. They take the pieces of leather that have been cut and set about stitching and hammering and sewing. Their quick and skillful work amazes the shoemaker

and his wife. The little men do not cease until all the leather is transformed into shoes. When they are done, they run away just as quickly as they arrived.

The next morning, the shoemaker's wife is filled with gratitude and wants to express her thanks to the little men that had helped them. She suggests that because the little men are naked, they are probably cold and might appreciate some clothing. She decides to make the little men shirts, coats, pants, vests, and warm socks. She asks her husband to make them each a tiny pair of shoes. He gladly agrees, and they begin creating a wardrobe for the tiny men. On the night that all the tiny clothes and shoes are finished,

The shoemaker's wife spins new clothes for the little helpers.

they set the clothes and shoes out on the workbench instead of the previously cut leather. Once more they conceal themselves in the hiding place and wait for the little men. Promptly at midnight, the men come running in, excited to begin their work. When they find the beautiful little articles of clothing, they are surprised and delighted. They quickly dress themselves and begin to sing, "Now we are boys so fine to see / Why should we longer cobblers be?" As they sing, they dance and hop and twirl out of the shoemaker's house and never come again, but the shoemaker lives a happy and prosperous life from then on.

Emblematic Elves

This tale is considered to be **emblematic**, or representative, of elf behavior because it includes many of the common beliefs regarding elves. For example, the elves are industrious workers in this story. They appear regularly at the same time of night and work at an astonishing rate, much like elves from a variety of other, more ancient myths. The elves in this story are also tiny and are hidden from the unsuspecting eye. Their changing visibility within this story strikes an interesting balance between myths that assert that elves are simply tiny and others that insist they are (or can become) invisible. The elves in this story are also incredibly charitable. They work quickly and carefully for the shoemaker without expecting anything in return. This benevolence reflects the characteristics of light elves from Norse mythology, working tirelessly in order to bring others happiness. Their abrupt departure at the end of the tale is also a common occurrence in elf folklore, along with the grateful human experiencing a happy and successful life after interacting with elves.

The Rest of the Picture

"The Shoemaker and the Elves" is the longest of the Grimm fairy tales in which elves feature. However, as mentioned previously, the brothers Grimm included two other tales about elves in their stories. One tale is about a young servant girl who is asked to be the godmother of a baby to be baptized. She is hesitant, but the elves convince her to participate in the ceremony. They take her into a hollow mountain, where she takes part in the baptism and the following ceremony. Shortly after the celebration, the girl wishes to go home, but the elves beg her to stay three days with them. She agrees, and in those three days, the elves play and laugh with her, doing everything they can to make her happy. At the end of the three days, they fill her pockets with gold and send her on her way, back home. Once she leaves she discovers she has not been away for three days, as she thought, but seven years.

The third elf story relates the tale of a woman who has had her child taken out of its crib and replaced with a **changeling**. The mother consults a neighbor, who instructs her to put the child in front of a fire and boil water in two eggshells. The woman does as she is told, and immediately the child is overtaken with laughter. The instant he begins to chuckle, a group of elves rush in with the woman's child, set it down, and rush back out, taking the changeling with them.

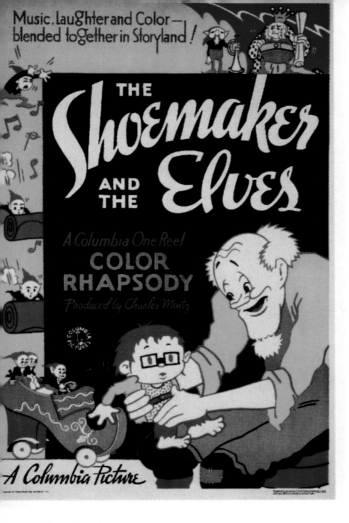

There have been many interpretations of "The Shoemaker and the Elves."

While these stories are also among the lore of elves, they paint the elf as more of a devilish trickster than a kind, playful assistant. Over the years, the characteristics of elves have been defined by illustrations that more closely resemble the elves in "The Shoemaker and the Elves," thus it is the more influential and consequential fairy tale.

Modern-Day Interpretations

Over time, "The Shoemaker and the Elves" has inspired a number of interpretations of the myth in popular culture. Many of these interpretations have been in the form of cartoons. In 1946, Friz Freleng, an American animator, created a musical adaptation of "The Shoemaker and the Elves" called *Holiday for Shoestrings*. Freleng's animation featured a crowd of elves as opposed to only two featured in the original telling. Ten years later, in 1956, Looney Tunes released the cartoon *Yankee Dood It*, which featured Elmer Fudd as king of the elves, returning to the shoemaker in order to give him a lesson.

Elf Music

A commonly told myth about elf behavior is that they love music and dancing. Many tales feature elves frolicking, making music, and dancing in nature. It is said that elves love to dance in the meadows, especially at night. They form a circle and often hold hands while dancing.

Although most humans do not observe elves dancing, it is said that you can tell when elves have been dancing in the meadows because the grass where their tiny feet have touched is softer and greener. If any human sees their dancing and stands in the middle of their circle, magical happenings occur. Some traditions maintain that the human who perceives the elf dance from the center of the ring simply enjoys their favor and has a splendid evening, while others maintain that the human will die.

Many cultures believe that elves are expert musicians and that any man who hears the music of the elf and tries to play it himself will find that he is incapable of stopping and will play until he dies of exhaustion. The only way for a musician to escape this horrible fate is to play the tune backwards or have someone cut the strings of their instrument as they play. This last remedy is complicated by the belief that anyone who hears the elf music being reproduced will find themselves in a state of frenzied dancing, which they cannot stop as long as the music is played.

ELVES AND HUMANS

"A world in which elves exist and magic works offers greater opportunities to digress and explore."

TERRY BROOKS

WHILE ELVES HAVE THE CAPABILITY of being either good or mischievous, their interactions with humans are generally characterized as positive. In the majority of myths where humans and elves interact, elves are described as rewarding the good deeds of humans.

The Fisherman and the Elf

One such myth tells of a peasant fisherman who happens upon a man trying to free his horse, which has gotten stuck in a bog. The fisherman stops and assists the stranger. The stranger thanks the man and says that he does not have money to pay him. Instead, he can offer the assurance that the fisherman will always catch fish

Opposite: A rare human observer joins an elf dance.

whenever he goes to sea, as long as the fisherman does not go out to sea before he sees the stranger pass his house, heading toward the shore. The fisherman follows the stranger's advice, and for three years he waits to see the man pass, then goes out to sea, and comes back home with more fish than he can eat.

One day, the fisherman looks out his window and sees that the weather is favorable for fishing. However, he does not see the stranger pass his house. He waits and waits, and finally grows impatient and heads toward the shore. When he gets to the water's edge he cannot find his boat and thus is kept from fishing. Later that evening, there is a terrible storm, and all the boats that are out to sea are wrecked and sunk, drowning all the other fishermen.

That night as the surviving fisherman sleeps, the stranger comes to him in a dream and tells him that he had kept him from going out to sea even though the fisherman did not follow his advice, thus saving his life. He tells the fisherman never to wait for him to pass his house again, as they will never see each other again.

Another tale that details elf gratitude is one of a peasant's wife, who dreams that an elf woman visits her bedside. The elf woman begs her to leave 2 quarts (1.9 liters) of milk in a corner of her house every day so that she can feed her child. The woman promises to do what the elf woman asks, and when she awakens, she decides to keep her promise. Every day for a month she places a bowl of milk in the corner the elf woman had pointed out, and every evening she finds the bowl empty. Finally, after a month has passed, the elf woman returns to her dreams and thanks her, telling her to accept the token of her appreciation that she will find in her bed when she wakes up. The next morning, the woman finds a beautiful silver belt beneath her pillow.

Mischievous Visitors

While many of the most popular tales of elves describe generous, grateful beings, most people were cautious when it came to the powers of elves and attributed curious happenings to the magic of elves. In olden times, it was common for people to take precautions in order to **appease** the mysterious beings.

In Europe, elves were often said to visit human dwellings in secret and cause a variety of disturbances in the household. They were said to enjoy creating knots and tangles in the manes and tails of horses. Farmers referred to these knots as elf-locks, and when the tangles were discovered, it was often said that horses had been elf-ridden in the night. Elves were also blamed when milk turned sour and were even thought to be able to give nightmares by sitting on people's heads while they slept. In fact, a German word for nightmare is *alptraum*, which translates to "elf dream." In order to prevent bad dreams, many people believed that you simply had to stuff the keyholes of your bedroom door with tissue to prevent the elves from entering.

Elves are playful and love to cause mischief in human houses.

Some households had images of elves carved onto doors or gates as a means of protection.

Before people had a way of explaining mental and physical illnesses, elves were said to be the source of madness and mysterious disease. It was thought that elves could cause deep sadness or joy in humans at will. For this reason, young men were warned they should never be tempted by beautiful young women, as those women may be elves seeking to drive them mad. Many people also believed that elves could cause sickness in cattle if they grazed in any area where elves had been. If cattle did stray into elf territory, the cure for illnesses was eating a handful of St. John's wort, which had been plucked at midnight on St. John's Night (June 23), a celebratory evening in honor of the summer solstice.

For a time, Scandinavian and German households worshipped elves as their protectors. Images of various elves were often carved on doorposts, gates, and pillars. Sacrifices were offered to elves in order to appease the playful beings. Sometimes these sacrifices were of a small animal. A bowl of milk, porridge, or honey might be offered to the unseen spirits as well. These offerings became known as *Alf-blot*.

Though there were a variety of measures taken to ensure that elves did not disturb households, they were generally considered charitable, sometimes playful beings that rewarded good behavior and played tricks on those that were in the wrong. Elves could certainly be tricksters, but they were very rarely considered malevolent beings.

An elf's front door.

Construction in Iceland

In Iceland, there is a continued debate about both the existence of elves and the best way to appease the tiny creatures said to live in the hills. Protests often arise in an effort to stop construction projects that might disturb the elves. The argument about the existence and protection of elves rages so consistently that the Icelandic Road and Coastal Administration has a lengthy standard response for press **inquiries** about elves. A portion of the statement reads:

> We value the heritage of our ancestors and if oral tradition passed on from one generation to the other tells us that a certain location is cursed, or that supernatural beings inhabit a certain rock, then this must be considered a cultural treasure. In the days when the struggle with the forces of nature was harsher than it is now, conservation came to the fore in this folklore, and copses and beautiful natural features were even spared.
>
> The reaction of the [administration] to these concerns has varied. Issues have been settled by delaying the construction project at a certain point whilst the elves living there have supposedly moved on. At other places the people in charge have seen no other solution than to continue the project against the wishes of certain individuals. There have been occasions when working arrangements have been changed slightly but at little extra expense.

ELVES ACROSS THE GLOBE

"Loud from the hills the voice of riot comes,
Where Yumboes shout and beat their Jaloff drums."

THOMAS KEIGHTLEY,

THE WORLD GUIDE TO GNOMES, FAIRIES, ELVES AND OTHER LITTLE PEOPLE

WHILE THE VAST MAJORITY OF ELVEN lore originated in Scandinavia, similar creatures are present in folktales in different societies around the world. These creatures are not mirror images of elves but do share many similarities with elvenkind.

YUMBOES OF WEST AFRICA

West African mythology tells of a race of creatures called Yumboes. They are around 2 feet (0.6 meters) tall and have white coloring, and their hair is said to be silver. Yumboes are attached to certain families and love music and dancing. When a member

Opposite:
The Jinn, or genie, is a creature of Arabian mythology.

of the family passes away, they are said to be heard grieving and dancing on the deceased's graves. Yumboes live underground in the Paps hills. Their dwelling is quite luxurious, and many stories about them concern travelers who had been invited into their underground home and entertained. These mischievous creatures come out at night to play tricks on the natives. They steal corn that the women grind in mortars and are seen fishing from canoes in the bay. After roasting their fish in the fires set by the natives, they drink palm wine until they are intoxicated, then they dance and beat their drums.

The Shedeem

Jewish belief tells of beings known as the Shedeem or Mazikeen. The Shedeem are believed to be Adam's children, who were birthed when Adam was exiled from the Garden of Eden. The Shedeem are invisible, winged, and clairvoyant. They are also able to shapeshift, and their stories often have a moral about the pitfalls of temptation.

One such tale of the Shedeem relates the story of a greedy old man who is taken to a dwelling within a mountain by a male stranger. The inhabitants of the mountainside habitat strike the visitor as being quite odd and unlike humans. A weeping woman informs the man that he should not accept any food or drink from his hosts under any circumstances. The strange man offers the visitor food, but he refuses. The visitor is then led throughout the cave to rooms that contain many riches. Despite the temptations, the visitor refuses to accept his host's offerings, and instead pleads to be taken back to his family. Finally, the visitor spots a ring of keys that looks exactly like his own keys.

The strange man says that they are his keys and gives them to the visitor, telling him that from now on his greedy heart will be open to the poor. He commands the visitor to shut his eyes and instantly transports him back home to his family, where he spends the rest of his life fulfilled as a result of helping others.

The Iron-Fearing Jinn

Arabian mythology tells of beings called the Jinn. Much like the elves of Norse mythology, they can have either a benevolent or **malignant** disposition. Both kinds of Jinn are organized into communities and are governed by princes. They are said to have formed from a smokeless fire thousands of years before Adam. The fire from which they were formed circulates through their bodies. When they are wounded, this fire is released, and they are burned to ash.

They sometimes procreate with humans, and their offspring shares characteristics with both species. They can assume either visible or invisible form at will, and they can also appear as humans or animals, most often becoming serpents, cats, or dogs. One weakness that the Jinn are believed to have is a fear of iron. When in human form, the good Jinn is usually considered to be very attractive, while their evil counterparts are often seen as hideous, sometimes of **gargantuan** proportion.

When a whirlwind causes giant pillars of sand to form and whip across the desert, they are said to be caused by the flying evil Jinn. Some Arabs yell "Iron!" or "God is great!" when they see these pillars in the hopes that they will **dissipate**.

The "Little Monk" of Naples

The residents of Naples, Italy, believe in a short, fat little man they call Monaciello, or "Little Monk." He dresses in monk robes and sometimes wears a large hat. Though the location of the Monaciello is not known, many believe he dwells in the remains of abbeys and monasteries that sit atop the hills. He is also considered to be very familiar with the underground passages of Naples. While the citizens of Naples generally consider interactions with Monaciello to be desirable, he is said to have a mischievous streak, like elves. Some say he is a playful trickster who pulls people's clothes off and steals bedspreads. Monaciello reveals himself to people late at night and silently encourages them to follow him. The lucky people who are curious and courageous enough to obey are led to hidden treasures and become very wealthy. Monaciello is said only to assist those who are most in need and who have done all they can to provide for themselves. Once someone has a visit from Monaciello, their fortunes reverse immediately. For this reason, when someone comes into a large sum of money it is common for the residents of Naples to comment, "Perhaps he has had the Little Monk in his house."

Christmas Elves in Norway

While many cultures leave cookies for Santa Claus on Christmas Eve, the people of Denmark leave treats for a different kind of visitor. The Nisse is said to live in the lofts of barns and assist with chores as long as the farmers treat him well. He is described as a short, old man who wears grey clothes and a red hat. He expects a large bowl of porridge with a pat of butter on Christmas Eve in return for his help with the livestock. Many families also leave the leftovers from their Christmas dinner out so the Nisse can partake in what is left of the feast.

While the Nisse enjoy helping farmers, he is quick to anger and plays tricks if he does not believe he is being treated well. One tale tells of the Nisse finding porridge on Christmas Eve without butter in it. He is so enraged that he kills the farmer's milking cow that is sleeping in the barn. He grows hungry and decides to eat the porridge anyway, only to find that the farmer has placed the butter on the bottom of the bowl. The Nisse is so overwhelmed with guilt that he steals the neighbor farm's milking cow to replace the one he foolishly slaughtered.

ELVES ARE HERE TO STAY

"I just like to smile. Smiling's my favorite!"
BUDDY, *ELF*

WHILE IT WOULD SEEM LIKE A TINY creature present in ancient fairy tales might not have much influence on today's culture, nothing could be further from the truth. Elf mythology lives on through modern belief and imagination. The cherished image of elves still inspires great feeling and interest in people around the world.

MAINSTAY OF ICELANDIC CULTURE

Though most cultures now look upon the elf as a representation of nature or a festive holiday image, a surprising number of Icelandic people still harbor a sincere belief in and deep reverence for elves.

Icelandic elves are referred to as *Huldufólk*, or hidden people. While the exact number of Icelandic people who believe in elves is debatable, there are enough believers to make the

Opposite: Will Ferrell's Buddy the Elf is just one of many beloved modern elves.

55

establishment of an elf tourism industry necessary. Several tourist sites, such as the Elfschool, offer tours riddled with elf facts and folklore.

The Elfschool, located in Reykjavik, is an institution that offers visitors a chance to learn all about elves. Their website explains some of the things visitors will learn: "about hundreds of Icelanders that have had personal contact with the elves themselves, and many of them have been invited into the homes of the elves and the hidden people in Iceland, and have often eaten food there and sometimes also slept there during one or more nights." In addition, the Elfschool offers an immersion course about Iceland elves, complete with a study book. In each class, students listen to tales about elves rescuing humans, and come to understand how the elf–human relationship has evolved throughout the centuries and continues today. Other attractions, such as Icelandic Wonders, a small museum in Stokkseyri, also offer a glimpse into the world of Icelandic elves.

In addition to tourism, elves influence other industries. Various construction projects around Iceland, for example, have been plagued by mysterious mechanical failures and delays that are said to have been caused by the Huldufólk. Several projects have been met with protests. Civilians accuse certain projects of threatening areas where elves are believed to reside. In various parts of the countryside, tiny colorful elf doors can be seen leaning against rocks, marking their domain.

ELVES IN POPULAR CULTURE

Though elves began appearing in the folklore of the Norsemen, their images are still much loved today. They have inspired a variety

of fantasy characters and have contributed greatly to our modern Christmas celebrations.

Representations of elves in popular culture range widely from Christmas traditions to fantasy books to Disney movies. Several Christmas movies spotlight elf characters, including the 1964 television special *Rudolph the Red-Nosed Reindeer*, which features Hermey the Elf, who wants to leave the North Pole and become a dentist. A more recent depiction of the Christmas elf is portrayed in the 2003 movie *Elf*, which stars Will Ferrell as Buddy, a human who is raised as an elf and journeys to America from the North Pole in order to find his birth parents. With his light-hearted hijinks and Christmas spirit, Buddy is able to show his father, a jaded businessman, the true meaning of Christmas.

Another Christmas elf seen around the holiday season is the elf on the shelf. *The Elf on the Shelf* is a children's storybook published in 2004 by Carol Aebersold and her two daughters, Chanda Bell and Christa Pitts. The book tells the tale of an Aebersold family tradition. An elf is adopted by a family and named. The elf watches over the family and reports back to the North Pole every night in order to tell Santa who is naughty and who is nice.

Each morning the elf returns to the house in a new location for children to discover. Each copy of the book comes with an elf figurine that looks like the one in the book, which the parents can move from place to place at night. The success of the book has spawned a half-hour animated Christmas story entitled *An Elf Story*, which premiered in 2001, and a Macy's Thanksgiving Day Parade balloon that made its debut in 2012. The elf on the shelf phenomenon has also birthed a few mobile apps. One is a hide and seek game where players scan their screens to find the hidden elf on the shelf. In recent years, people have begun taking photos of children and even adults posing as the elf on the shelf.

ELVES IN BOOKS, ON TV, AND IN FILM

In addition to Christmas traditions, elves have had great influence on fantasy books and role playing games. One wildly popular book and movie series featuring elves is the *Harry Potter* series by J.K. Rowling. Rowling's elves are house elves, ugly bony beings that stand about 3 feet (1 m) tall and wear old linens (such as old pillowcases) as clothing. These house elves are not immortal but grow quite old. They have long ears, high-pitched voices, large eyes, and speak of themselves in the third person. The house elves in the Harry Potter books and movies are extremely obedient and are usually happy serving their masters. This is a good thing, since they will typically spend their entire lifetime in the service of others.

Another very popular modern representation of elvenkind can be found in the Peter Jackson film trilogy *The Lord of the Rings*, based on the trilogy of books by the same name. The elves in these movies were incredibly popular characters. Played by actors such as Orlando Bloom, Liv Tyler, and Cate Blanchett, the elves in these films inspired a whole new generation to believe in these pointy-eared, nature-loving creatures. *The Lord of the Rings* films have grossed many millions of dollars in ticket sales worldwide and have a multitude of accompanying merchandise, including toys, board games, clothing, and jewelry.

Elves have even appeared on television. The most popular elves on television are the Keebler elves, mascots of the Keebler Company, the largest cookie and cracker manufacturer in the United States. The Keebler Company began advertising their cookies using elves back in 1969. J.J. Keebler was introduced as the first head elf and later Ollie, a fun-loving golf enthusiast elf, portrayed the role. Finally, in 1970, Ernie J. Keebler, sporting a green coat, red hat, and yellow tie, assumed the position of head elf and has held it ever since. The Keebler elves make their treats in the Hollow Tree, which is said to house magic ovens that produce the delicious cookies, crackers, and ice cream cones. Ernie is not alone in his quest to make "uncommonly good" food. Over the years, Keebler has introduced viewers to a variety of Hollow Tree workers. For instance, Buckets is the elf in charge of pouring chocolate fudge onto cookies, Fast Eddie wraps the finished products, and Elwood is a speedy elf who prepares the dough by running through it. Keebler elves are immortal and no one knows how long they have been baking their tasty treats. Hopefully, they will continue for years to come.

The image of the elf has transformed over the years. From the Norse myths of Vikings to Orlando Bloom on the big screen as Legolas in *The Lord of the Rings*, elves have inhabited a great variety of forms, occupations, and personalities. With such a rich history of images and storytelling, you can rest assured that tales of elves will continue to be passed down for many more generations.

GLOSSARY

appease To do something to satisfy someone or something.

basis Something that acts as the foundation, generally for an idea or argument.

benevolence Showing kindness.

changeling A strange child substituted by elves for a human child.

charitable Generous.

clairvoyance The ability to see the future or read minds.

dissipate Disappear.

emblematic Symbolic of or representing something.

gargantuan Very large.

homely Plain or ugly in appearance.

inadvertently Without intending to; accidentally.

inhospitable Harsh or unwelcoming.

inquiries Formal questions.

malignant Harmful.

Norsemen Members of a medieval Scandinavian group of people.

obscurity State of being hidden; unknown.

Tarnkappe A small, red hat worn by dwarves that protects them from turning to stone in the sunlight.

To Learn More About Elves

Books

Grimm, Jacob and Wilhelm. *The Complete Grimm's Fairy Tales.* New York: Pantheon, 1944.

Guerber, H.A. *Myths of Norsemen From the Eddas and Sagas.* New York: Dover, 1992.

Keightley, Thomas. *The World Guide to Gnomes, Fairies, Elves, and Other Little People.* New York: Gramercy, 1978.

Website

The Elfschool

www.theelfschool.com/home

The official website of the Elfschool, an institution in Reykjavik, Iceland, that offers information and classes about Icelandic folklore and elf sightings.

Video

Holiday for Shoestrings

www.dailymotion.com/video/x15mqib_holiday-for-shoestrings_fun

The 1946 Merry Melodies cartoon based on "The Shoemaker and the Elves."

Bibliography

Booss, Claire. *Scandinavian Folk & Fairy Tales: Tales from Norway, Sweden, Denmark, Finland, Iceland.* New York: Avenel Books, 1984.

Christiansen, Reidar Thorwalf. *Folktales of Norway.* Chicago: University of Chicago Press, 1964.

Guerber, H. A. *Myths of the Norsemen: From the Eddas and the Sagas.* New York: Dover Publications, 1992.

Grimm, Jacob, and Wilhelm Grimm. *The Complete Grimm's Fairy Tales.* New York: Pantheon, 1972.

"Icelandic Wonders — Elves, Trolls, Myths, Folklore." *Icelandic Wonders.* Accessed December 19, 2015. http://www.icelandicwonders.com.

Jacobs, Ryan. "Why So Many Icelanders Still Believe in Invisible Elves." *The Atlantic,* October 29, 2013.

Keightley, Thomas. *The World Guide to Gnomes, Fairies, Elves, and Other Little People.* New York: Avenel Books, 1978.

"Mythical Creatures Guide: Elf." Accessed December 18, 2015. http://www.mythicalcreaturesguide.com/page/Elf.

Riordan, James. *An Illustrated Treasury of Fairy and Folk Tales.* Twickenham, UK: Hamlyn, 1986.

Zipes, Jack. *Spells of Enchantment: The Wondrous Fairy Tales of Western Culture.* New York: Viking, 1991.

Index

Page numbers in **boldface** are illustrations. Entries in **boldface** are glossary terms.

About the Author

Joel Newsome grew up traveling the country as a military child. He studied English at Western Michigan University in Kalamazoo, Michigan. He has earned fellowships from Cave Canem and VONA. He currently resides in Massachusetts where he teaches English to international students. So far, he has never seen an elf.